Collins

easy le

Phonics

Ages 5–6

owl

How to use this book

- Find a quiet, comfortable place to work, away from distractions.
- Tackle one topic at a time.
- Help with reading the instructions where necessary and ensure your child understands what to do.
- Encourage your child to check their own answers as they complete each activity.
- Discuss with your child what they have learnt.
- Let your child return to their favourite pages once they have been completed, to talk about the activities.
- Reward your child with plenty of praise and encouragement.

Special features

- Yellow boxes: Introduce a topic and outline the key focus.
- Red boxes: Emphasise a rule relating to the unit.

Parent tips

- It is vital that your child learns the correct sound for each of the letters taught in this book. This is very much a book you work through with your child; reinforce the correct letter sounds as they progress and help them with any language they may be unable to read.
- This table gives an example word for each sound in this book, so that you have a reference point for each correct sound.

Page 4	sun ant tap	Page 20	thin ring
Page 5	pea ink net	Page 21	tail weed
Page 7	mop dog goat	Page 22	light boat
Page 8	otter cat king	Page 23	moon car
Page 10	duck egg	Page 24	fort hurt
Page 11	up ring hat	Page 25	owl oil
Page 12	bed fish lamp	Page 26	fear stair
Page 14	jam van web	Page 27	sure ladder
Page 15	x-ray yellow zip	Page 28	ink hand
Page 17	puff bell boss	Page 29	clap
Page 18	buzz quiz	Page 30	trip
Page 19	rich sheep		

Published by Collins
An imprint of HarperCollinsPublishers
1 London Bridge Street
London SE1 9GF

Browse the complete Collins catalogue at www.collins.co.uk

First published in 2012

© HarperCollinsPublishers 2012
This edition © HarperCollinsPublishers 2015

15 14 13 12

ISBN 978-0-00-813435-8

British Library Cataloguing in Publication Data

A Catalogue record for this publication is available from the British Library

Page layout by Linda Miles, Lodestone Publishing and Contentra Technologies
Illustrated by Rachel Annie Bridgen, Jenny Tulip, Steve Evans, Kathy Baxendale and Andy Tudor
Cover design by Sarah Duxbury and Paul Oates
Cover illustration by Kathy Baxendale
Project managed by Katie Galloway and Sonia Dawkins

Printed in Great Britain by Martins the Printers

Contents

Letters s, a and t

Letter s

Say the letter.
Write the letter.

Write the missing letter.

_____un

_____ix

_____ock

Letter a

Say the letter.
Write the letter.

Circle the objects that begin with the letter **a**.

Letter t

Say the letter.
Write the letter.

Write the missing letter.

_____rain

_____ap

_____omato

Letters p, i and n

Letter p

Say the letter.
Write the letter.

p p

Circle the objects that begin with the letter **p**.

Letter i

Say the letter.
Write the letter.

i i

Write the missing letter.

_____nk   _____nsect   _____gloo

Letter n

Say the letter.
Write the letter.

n n

Add **n** to finish the words.

_____et   _____ose   _____est

Using letters s, a, t, p, i and n

You can make some words using the letters **s, a, t, p, i** and **n**.

p + i + n = pin

1 Do each word sum to make a word.

s + a + t = _____

s + i + p = _____

t + a + p = _____

p + a + n = _____

t + i + p = _____

p + a + t = _____

2 Write the words you have made in **1** under the right picture.

_____   _____   _____

_____   _____   _____

Letters m, d and g

Letter m

Say the letter.
Write the letter.

m m

Write the missing letter.

_____ouse _____op _____onkey

Letter d

Say the letter.
Write the letter.

d d

Cross out the object that does not start with **d**.

Letter g

Say the letter.
Write the letter.

g g

Add **g** to finish the words.

_____irl _____host _____ate

Letters o, c and k

Letter o

Say the letter.
Write the letter.

O   o   .   .   .   .

Add **o** to finish the words.

_____range

_____ctopus

_____tter

Letter c

Say the letter.
Write the letter.

C   c   .   .   .   .

Circle the objects that begin with the letter **c**.

Letter k

Say the letter.
Write the letter.

k   k   .   .   .   .

Write the missing letter.

_____ing

_____ite

_____ey

Using letters c, t, n, m, p, a and o

You can make some words using the letters **c, t, n, m, p, a** and **o**.

c + a + t = cat

1 Do each word sum to make a word.

c + a + p = _____

m + a + p = _____

m + a + n = _____

t + a + p = _____

c + a + n = _____

m + o + p = _____

2 Write the words you have made in **1** under the right picture.

_____   _____   _____

_____   _____   _____

Letters ck and e

Letters ck

Say the letters.
Write the letters.

1 Cross out the object that does not end with **ck**.

2 Write the missing **ck** letters to make the words.

du_____   clo_____   so_____

Letter e

Say the letter.
Write the letter.

1 Write the missing letter.

_____gg   _____lephant   _____nvelope

2 Draw a part of your arm that begins with **e**.

Letters u, r and h

Letter u

Say the letter.
Write the letter.

u   u   .   .   .   .

Cross out the object that does not start with **u**.

Letter r

Say the letter.
Write the letter.

r   r   .   .   .   .   .   .

Tick the objects that begin with the letter **r**.

Letter h

Say the letter.
Write the letter.

h   h   .   .   .   .   .

Write the missing letter.

_____at   _____en   _____orse

Letters b, f and l

Letter b

Say the letter.
Write the letter. b b

Circle the objects that begin with the letter **b**.

Letter f

Say the letter.
Write the letter. f f

Write the missing letter.

  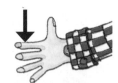

_____ish   _____eather   _____inger

Letter l

Say the letter.
Write the letter.

Add **l** to finish the words.

_____etter   _____amp   _____ion

Using letters l, g, p, t, r, n, e and a

You can make some words using the letters **l, g, p, t, r, n, e** and **a**.

p + e + g = **peg**

1 Do each word sum to make a word.

l + e + g = _____

r + a + t = _____

r + a + g = _____

p + e + t = _____

r + a + n = _____

p + a + n = _____

2 Write the words you have made in **1** under the right picture.

_____   _____   _____

_____   _____   _____

Letters j, v and w

Letter j

Say the letter.
Write the letter.

j j . . . .

Write the missing letter.

_____am

_____ug

_____elly

Letter v

Say the letter.
Write the letter.

V V . . . . . .

Circle the objects that begin with the letter **v**.

Letter w

Say the letter.
Write the letter.

W W . . . . . .

Write the missing letter.

_____orm

_____eb

_____indow

Letters x, y and z

Letter x

Say the letter.
Write the letter.

Write what this picture shows.

The word begins with **x**. _____

Letter y

Say the letter.
Write the letter.

Write the missing letter.

      _____oyo

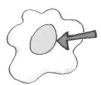   _____ellow

_____olk

Letter z

Say the letter.
Write the letter.

Cross out the object that does not start with **z**.

Using letters r, a, b, t, o, h, n, s, d, i, u and p

You can make some words using the letters **r, a, b, t, o, h, n, s, d, i, u** and **p**.

b + u + n = bun

1 Do each word sum to make a word.

h + i + t = _____

s + u + n = _____

p + o + t = _____

s + a + d = _____

r + u + n = _____

b + a + t = _____

2 Write the words you have made in **1** under the right picture.

_____   _____   _____

_____   _____   _____

Letters ff, ll and ss

These words end with the letters **ff**, **ll** or **ss**.

o**ff**　　　　　　fu**ll**　　　　　　ki**ss**

Say the words.

---

1 Write the word from the box that matches each picture.

> **bell**　　**mess**　　**hiss**　　**puff**　　**doll**　　**cuff**

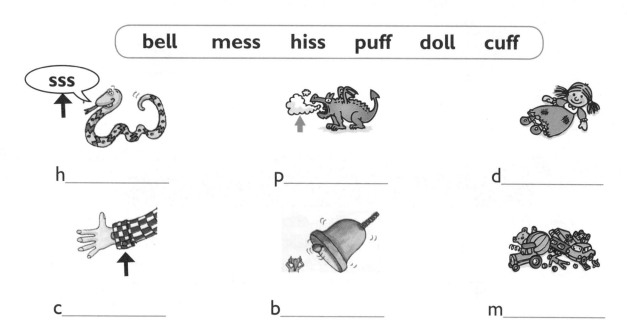

h_____　　　　　p_____　　　　　d_____

c_____　　　　　b_____　　　　　m_____

2 Add the correct letters (**ll** or **ss**) to finish the words.

te_____　　　　　bo_____　　　　　fu_____

le_____　　　　　se_____　　　　　ba_____

Letters zz and qu

Letters zz

Say the letters.
Write the letters.   ZZ ZZ · · · · · · · · · ·

1 Add **zz** to finish the words.

bu_____   ja_____   fu_____

2 Label the pictures with the correct words from **1**.

_____   _____

qu sound

Say the word. Listen to the **qu** sound.

quiz

> Remember **q** always has **u** after it.

1 Write the missing letters.

_____een   _____estion   _____ick

2 Draw and label a picture of an object that begins with **qu**.

ch and sh sounds

These words use **ch** or **sh** at the beginning or end of the word.

chips

fi**sh**

Say the words.

1 Write the word from the box that matches each picture.

> **sheep**   **rich**   **cheese**   **ship**

_____

_____

_____

_____

2 Finish the words by adding **ch** or **sh**.
The clues will help you.

You buy things from here.   _____op

You eat this in the middle of the day.   lun_____

You wear these on your feet.   _____oes

A baby hen.   _____ick

th and ng sounds

th sound

Say the word. Listen to the **th** sound.

think

1 Write the word from the box that matches each picture.

> **path   three   bath**

_____   _____   _____

2 Circle the **th** sound in each word in **1**.

ng sound

Say the word. Listen to the **ng** sound at the end of the word.

stro**ng**

1 Add **ing** or **ong** to finish these words.

l_____

r_____

s_____

w_____

k_____

2 + 2 = 3 ✗

wr_____

ai and ee sounds

These words use the **ai** or **ee** sounds in the middle of the word.

rain

feet

Say the words.
Listen to the sound the letters **ai** and **ee** make in the words.

---

1 Add **ai** or **ee** to finish these words.

n_____l   p_____l   b_____

s_____l   t_____l   ch_____se

2 Choose a word from the box to finish each of the sentences.

> **pain   wait   week   rain**

My dog loves the _____.

I had to _____ for my lunch.

It is my birthday in a _____.

I had a _____ in my tooth.

igh and oa sounds

igh sound

Say the word. Listen to the **igh** sound.

fl**igh**t

1 Write the word from the box that matches each picture.

| light   night   right |

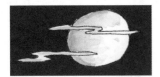

8+6=14 ✓

_____   _____   _____

2 Circle the **igh** sound in each word in **1**.

oa sound

Say the word. Listen to the **oa** sound.

g**oa**t

1 Choose an **oa** word from the box to finish each of the sentences.

| road   coat   toad |

The _____ jumped in the pond.

I walked up the _____.

I put on my _____.

2 Circle the **oa** sound in each word you have written in **1**.

oo and ar sounds

These words use the **oo** or **ar** sounds.

goo**se**

jar

Say the words.
Listen to the sound the letters **oo** and **ar** make in the words.

1 Add **oo** or **ar** to finish these words.

f_____d

c_____

r_____t

m_____n

c_____d

b_____k

2 Sort the words in the box into the table.

| park | zoo | hoof | hard | cart | boot |

oo words	**ar** words

or and ur sounds

These words use the **or** or **ur** sounds.

fork

burn

Say the words.
Listen to the sound the letters **or** and **ur** make in the words.

1 Add **or** or **ur** to finish these words.

t_____n   c_____k   h_____t

f_____t   f_____   s_____f

2 Choose an **or** or **ur** word from the box to finish each of the sentences.

born   fort   hurt   burns

We went to the _____.

Dad _____ the wood.

The foal was _____ in the shed.

Jess _____ her leg.

ow and oi sounds

Say the word. Listen to the **ow** sound.

cow

1 Write the word from the box that matches each picture.

clown owl brown

_____ _____ _____

2 Circle the **ow** sound in each word in **1**.

oi sound

Say the word. Listen to the **oi** sound.

boil

1 Choose an **oi** word from the box to finish each of the sentences.

coin soil oil

Dad put _____ in the car.

I found a _____ on the path.

I covered a seed with _____.

2 Circle the **oi** sound in each word you have written in **1**.

ear and air sounds

These words use the **ear** or **air** sounds.

ear   h**air**

Say the words.
Listen to the sound the letters **ear** and **air** make in the words.

1 Write the word from the box that matches each picture.

> fear   tear   beard   pair   stairs   chair

f_____   p_____   s_____

t_____   c_____   b_____

2 Add the correct letters, **ear** or **air**, to finish the words.

f_____   f_____   y_____   n_____

3 Add the word **ear** or **air** to each sentence.

My _____ hurts!

I need some fresh _____.

ure and er sounds

ure sound

Say the word. Listen to the **ure** sound.

man**ure**

1 Choose an **ure** word from the box to finish each of the sentences.

> manure   sure   cure

Are you _____ I can come for tea?

The doctor found a _____ for my sore foot.

I stepped in some horse _____!

2 Circle the **ure** sound in each word in **1**.

er sound

Say the word. Listen to the **er** sound.

lett**er**

Annie Jones
9 Little Street
Littleton

1 Circle the words that end in **er**.

ladder   tractor   summer

sailor   dinner   hammer

2 Write two more words that end in **er**.

_____   _____

nk and nd sounds

Say the words.
Listen to the sound the letters **nk** and **nd** make in the words.

sink

sand

1 Add **nk** or **nd** to finish these words.

po_____

wa_____

i_____

ha_____

be_____

pi_____

2 Choose an **nk** or **nd** word from the box to finish each of the sentences.

> **blink**　　**drink**　　**mend**　　**sand**

The sun made me _____.

Mum could not _____ my bike.

I love playing in the _____.

Aimee had a big _____.

l blends

Each of these words starts with an **l** blend.

blob   **cl**ap   **fl**ip   **pl**an

Say the words.

1 Add the correct **l** blend from the box to finish each word.

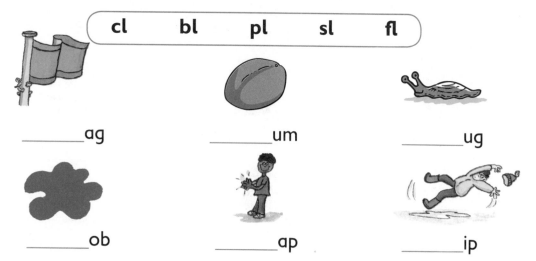

| cl | bl | pl | sl | fl |

_____ag

_____um

_____ug

_____ob

_____ap

_____ip

2 Write the words in the box into the table.

slam   flan   slid   club   flag   clip   plum   plug

cl words	**fl** words
pl words	**sl** words

3 Add words of your own to fill the gaps in the table in **2**.

r blends

Each of these words starts with an **r** blend.

drip   **fr**og   **tr**ip   **pr**am

Say the words.

1   Choose the correct **r** blend from the box to finish each word.

cr	dr	fr	gr	pr	tr

_____um   _____og   _____am

_____ab   _____ee   _____an

2   Write the words in the box into the table.

grin   crop   drip   trap   drop   trip   grab   crab

cr words	**dr** words
gr words	**tr** words

3   Add words of your own to fill the gaps in the table in **2**.

Top 12 words

It is very important to know how to read and spell these 12 words. You will find that these 12 words are used many times in your reading books.

and	**in**	**is**	**it**
that	**a**	**he**	**I**
of	**the**	**to**	**was**

1 Circle the 12 words from above in these sentences. One has been done for you.

(It) (was) (a) cold day.

Tom and Kim went in the shop.

Is it time to go?

I want that puppy.

He was on the swing.

2 Choose one of the 12 words to finish each sentence.

Dan went t____ Ali's house.

T_____ cat jumps i____ the bin.

What can h____ do?

I____ it time for lunch?

Answers

Letters s, a and t
Page 4

s   sun six sock

a   ant arrow (circled)

t   train tap tomato

Letters p, i and n
Page 5

p   pencil pear (circled)

i   ink insect igloo

n   net nose nest

Using letters s, a, t, p, i and n
Page 6

1   sat sip tap pan tip pat

2   sip tap pat sat pan tip

Letters m, d and g
Page 7

m   mouse mop monkey

d   feather (crossed out)

g   girl ghost gate

Letters o, c and k
Page 8

o   orange octopus otter

c   cat cup (circled)

k   king kite key

Using letters c, t, n, m, p, a and o
Page 9

1   cap map man tap can mop

2   mop cap can tap map man

Letters ck and e
Page 10

ck   1 mop (crossed out)

     2 duck clock sock

e   1 egg elephant envelope

    2 Picture of an elbow

Letters u, r and h
Page 11

u   cake (crossed out)

r   rabbit ring (ticked)

h   hat hen horse

Letters b, f and l
Page 12

b   bat ball (circled)

f   fish feather finger

l   letter lamp lion

Using letters l, g, p, t, r, n, e and a
Page 13

1   leg rat rag pet ran pan

2   leg ran pan rat pet rag

Letters j, v and w
Page 14

j   jam jug jelly

v   violin van (circled)

w   worm web window

Letters x, y and z
Page 15

x   x-ray

y   yoyo yellow yolk

z   rabbit (crossed out)

Using letters r, a, b, t, o, h, n, s, d, i, u and p
Page 16

1   hit sun pot sad run bat

2   sun bat pot sad hit run

Letters ff, ll and ss
Page 17

1   hiss puff doll cuff bell mess

2   tell boss full less sell ball

Letters zz and qu
Page 18

zz   1 buzz jazz fuzz

     2 jazz buzz

qu   1 queen question quick

     2 Child's picture of something beginning with **qu**

ch and sh sounds
Page 19

1   cheese ship rich sheep

2   shop lunch shoes chick

th and ng sounds
Page 20

th   1 three bath path

     2 three bath path

ng   long ring song **or** sing wing king wrong

ai and ee sounds
Page 21

1   nail peel bee sail tail cheese

2   My dog loves the **rain**.

     I had to **wait** for my lunch.

It is my birthday in a **week**.

I had a **pain** in my tooth.

igh and oa sounds
Page 22

igh   1 night right light

      2 night right light

oa   1 The **toad** jumped in the pond.

     I walked up the **road**.

     I put on my **coat**.

    2 toad

      road

      coat

oo and ar sounds
Page 23

1   food car root moon card bark

2

oo words	ar words
zoo	park
hoof	hard
boot	cart

or and ur sounds
Page 24

1   torn cork hurt fort fur surf

2   We went to the **fort**.

    Dad **burns** the wood.

    The foal was **born** in the shed.

    Jess **hurt** her leg.

ow and oi sounds
Page 25

ow   1 owl brown clown

     2 owl brown clown

oi   1 Dad put **oil** in the car.

     I found a **coin** on the path.

     I covered a seed with **soil**.

    2 oil

      coin

      soil

ear and air sounds
Page 26

1   fear pair stairs tear chair beard

2   fear fair year near

3   My **ear** hurts!

    I need some fresh **air**.